A TRUE BOOK™

The Most Endangered
Gorillas

Purchased from
Multnomah County Library
Title Wave Used Bookstore
216 NE Knott St, Portland, OR
503-988-5021

KATIE MARSICO

Children's Press®
An Imprint of Scholastic Inc.

Content Consultant
Dr. Stephen S. Ditchkoff
Professor of Wildlife Sciences
Auburn University, Auburn, Alabama

Library of Congress Cataloging-in-Publication Data
Names: Marsico, Katie, 1980– author.
Title: Gorillas / by Katie Marsico.
Other titles: Gorillas | True book.
Description: New York, NY : Children's Press, an imprint of Scholastic Inc., 2017. | Series: A true
    book | Includes bibliographical references and index.
Identifiers: LCCN 2016025110| ISBN 9780531227282 (library binding) | ISBN 9780531232798 (pbk.)
Subjects: LCSH: Gorilla—Juvenile literature. | Gorilla—Conservation—Juvenile literature. |
    Endangered species—Juvenile literature.
Classification: LCC QL737.P94 M3735 2017 | DDC 599.884—dc23
LC record available at https://lccn.loc.gov/2016025110

No part of this publication may be reproduced in whole or in part, or stored in a retrieval system,
or transmitted in any form or by any means, electronic, mechanical, photocopying, recording, or
otherwise, without written permission of the publisher. For information regarding permission,
write to Scholastic Inc., Attention: Permissions Department, 557 Broadway, New York, NY 10012.

© 2017 Scholastic Inc.
All rights reserved. Published in 2017 by Children's Press, an imprint of Scholastic Inc.
Printed in China 62
SCHOLASTIC, CHILDREN'S PRESS, A TRUE BOOK™, and associated logos are trademarks and/or
registered trademarks of Scholastic Inc.
1 2 3 4 5 6 7 8 9 10 R 26 25 24 23 22 21 20 19 18 17

Front cover: A gorilla in the jungle
Back cover: A silverback gorilla

Find the Truth!

Everything you are about to read is true *except* for one of the sentences on this page.

Which one is **TRUE**?

T or F Not all types of gorillas are endangered.

T or F A dangerous virus is a major threat to gorillas.

Find the answers in this book.

3

Contents

THE BIG TRUTH!

Learn the Lingo!

An eastern lowland gorilla
mother and her baby

A child checks out a gorilla at a zoo.

4 A Chance to Change the Story

What are people doing to protect gorillas?...... **33**

An adult male gorilla beats its chest.

Mount Sabyinyo is an extinct, or inactive, volcano that rises nearly 12,000 feet (3,658 meters) above Virunga National Park.

CHAPTER 1

A Rain Forest Rescue

Deep in the rain forests of central Africa, about 880 mountain gorillas are struggling to survive. Some make their home in Virunga National Park, a protected area of rain forest in the Democratic Republic of the Congo (DNC). But they still face many dangers. Ndakasi (en-dah-KAH-see), a baby gorilla, was born there in 2007. When she was just two months old, **poachers** killed her mother.

Virunga National Park is the oldest national park on the African continent.

ATLANTIC

AFRICA

OCEAN

★ Virunga National Park

Poachers sometimes use snares made of wire, which wrap around a gorilla's leg or arm.

Animals at Risk

Authorities suspected the person who attacked Ndakasi and her mother was linked to the illegal charcoal industry in Virunga National Park. People cut down trees in the park and elsewhere and use the wood to make charcoal. Charcoal is specially processed wood, bone, or other matter that is used as fuel. Many people in the country use charcoal to cook food and heat their homes. Some people in the charcoal trade kill gorillas as revenge against park rangers working against the industry.

After poachers killed her mother, Ndakasi was on her own. Too young to feed and defend herself, the young gorilla was certain to die. Fortunately, rangers found her and rushed her to Gorilla Doctors. This **conservation** organization has an international veterinary team. They provide treatment to injured, sick, and orphaned gorillas. Over time, veterinarians and rangers nursed Ndakasi back to health. Today, she lives alongside other orphaned gorillas at a **sanctuary** in Virunga National Park.

People with Gorilla Doctors have helped save many orphaned gorillas.

Powerful Primates

Gorillas like Ndakasi are the largest of the primates. Primates are a group of mammals that includes apes, such as gorillas, monkeys, and believe it or not—humans! In fact, gorillas are among humans' closest living relatives.

Most gorillas live in the forests of central and western Africa. They are known for their size and strength. These apes are also famous for their amazing gentleness and ability to express emotion.

Gorilla Range

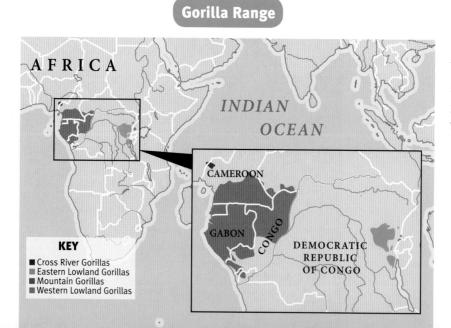

This map shows where gorillas live in the wild.

AFRICA

INDIAN OCEAN

CAMEROON

GABON

CONGO

DEMOCRATIC REPUBLIC OF CONGO

KEY
- Cross River Gorillas
- Eastern Lowland Gorillas
- Mountain Gorillas
- Western Lowland Gorillas

A large male gorilla charges to protect his troop, or group.

Destined to Disappear?

In the wild, gorillas have few natural enemies — except the occasional leopard or crocodile. But human activities such as poaching and illegal capture for the wildlife trade threaten their survival in a big way. So do **deforestation** and disease.

All gorillas are either endangered or critically endangered. Those that are endangered face a very high risk of **extinction**. For critically endangered gorillas, the threat of disappearing from the planet is even greater.

An eastern lowland gorilla baby holds on to its mother.

CHAPTER 2

Amazing Apes

Scientists estimate that between 100,000 and 200,000 gorillas live in the wild. Conservationists predict that this could change. They say that by the mid-2020s gorillas may no longer exist within much of their current habitat.

There are two main species of gorillas: eastern gorillas and western gorillas. Eastern lowland gorillas and mountain gorillas are **subspecies** of the first group. Western lowland gorillas and Cross River gorillas are subspecies of the second.

Baby gorillas don't crawl until they are two months old.

Physical Features

All gorillas have several features in common. These include a broad chest and shoulders, and a bulging stomach and forehead. Their hairless face features small eyes and a flattened nose.

Gorillas walk both on all fours and upright on their hind limbs. They have large hands and muscular arms and legs. In terms of upper-body strength, they're six times as powerful as humans!

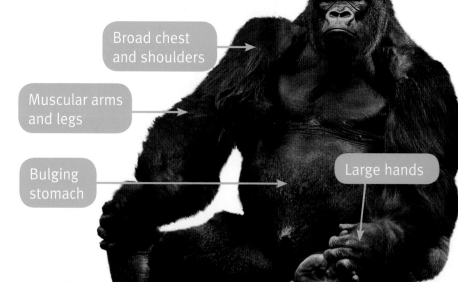

Male gorillas, like this one, are generally about two times heavier than females.

Small eyes, flattened nose

Hairless face, bulging forehead

Broad chest and shoulders

Muscular arms and legs

Bulging stomach

Large hands

A mountain gorilla munches on a snack.

Adult gorillas typically weigh between 158 and 484 pounds (70 and 220 kilograms). When standing upright, most are 4 to 6 feet (1.2 to 1.8 meters) tall. These stocky animals have dark skin, and hair that is various shades of black, brown, and gray.

Like humans, gorillas have 32 teeth. They mainly feed on fruit, leaves, shoots, stems, and roots. Some gorillas gobble up insects as well.

Telling Gorillas Apart

There are slight differences in diet, appearance, and habitat among gorilla subspecies.

Species	Weight (Adults)	Habitats	Distinguishing Features (Compared to Other Subspecies)
A COMPARISON OF GORILLA SUBSPECIES			
Cross River gorilla	Roughly 400 pounds (180 kg) on average	Tropical and subtropical rain forests found in mountainous areas	Smaller skull and teeth, shorter hands and feet
Eastern lowland gorilla	176 to 484 pounds (80 to 220 kg)	Tropical and subtropical moist forests found in the area drained by the Congo River	Stockier body, larger hands, and shorter nose and mouth
Mountain gorilla	300 to 425 pounds (136 to 193 kg)	Tropical and subtropical moist forests found in mountainous areas	Fur that tends to be far thicker
Western lowland gorilla	158 to 374 pounds (72 to 170 kg)	Tropical and subtropical moist forests found in coastal regions and the area drained by the Congo River	Smaller build and ears, wider skull, more noticeable brow ridges, fur on the head, limbs, and back that is more brown-gray in color, and fur on the chest that is more reddish brown in color

Big Thinkers

Scientists consider gorillas to be fairly intelligent. One sign of intelligence is the ability to solve problems creatively. A good indicator of this is whether an animal uses tools. Like many other primates, gorillas can use simple tools. People have photographed these apes dipping sticks in water to determine

Gorillas make tools out of materials that are readily available, such as sticks or rocks.

how deep the water is. Conservationists have even reported gorillas taking apart traps set by hunters.

Forest Families

Gorillas live in groups, called troops, of 2 to 50 members. An adult male is always the leader. This dominant, or lead, gorilla protects the troop. He also decides when and where members feed and sleep.

Gorillas spend most of their time eating and resting. These apes are more active during daylight hours. At night, they sleep in nests made out of leaves and branches.

Adult male gorillas have silver fur on their back. As a result, they are often called silverbacks.

A mountain gorilla rests in its nest during the day.

Gorilla Talk

Gorillas don't have an identifiable language like people do. Scientists believe they communicate by making at least 22 unique sounds. These include grunts, barks, screams, and cries. Other forms of communication involve facial expressions, movements, and even body odors. These allow troop members to share information about everything from food to danger to social status.

A gorilla mother interacts with her young offspring.

A Look at Life Cycle

In the wild, gorillas have a life span of up to 40 years. Females are generally ready to **reproduce** at the age of seven or eight. But, males often don't reproduce until they're about 15.

A mother gorilla is pregnant for about 8.5 months, and generally gives birth to one baby at a time. Youngsters are playful and often ride on their mothers' backs. They generally nurse, or drink milk from their mother, for two to three years.

Sign Language for Apes

Koko is no ordinary western lowland gorilla. Beginning in 1972, researchers in California have worked with Koko to teach her American Sign Language (ASL). She continues learning today! Koko's current vocabulary includes more than 1,100 signs. Sometimes she relies on ASL to express basic ideas such as "food" and "more." In other cases, Koko communicates emotions like sadness and love. This remarkable ape has even used ASL to create signs of her own!

Koko

Seed Spreaders

Gorillas have a big impact on animals outside of their troop. In fact, their survival is important to their entire **ecosystem**. Since a gorilla's diet is plant-based, its droppings contain seeds and other plant parts. As a result, when gorillas produce waste, they spread seeds. This leads to new plant growth within Africa's forests. Many other animals rely on these plants to survive. Elephants, okapi, and monkeys are just a few examples!

Okapi are one of the many animals that benefit from gorillas.

A woman sits next to a mountain gorilla.

A Common Code

Gorillas are also extremely important to people. These primates share more than 98 percent of their **genetic code** with humans. By studying gorillas, therefore, it's possible scientists will learn more about the human species. Why did people develop a more complex language than gorillas? Why do humans suffer from certain diseases that don't affect apes? The answers to such questions will be harder to find if gorillas become extinct!

Learn the Lingo!

PARDON ME!

Did someone belch? Gorillas frequently make a noise that sounds a lot like a burp. Yet the "belch call" isn't mainly about digestion. According to experts, this sound is similar to making a peace sign. It's another way of saying, "Don't worry! I'm not a threat!"

STRENGTH AND SIZE

In movies, gorillas are often shown beating their chests. But what does this gesture mean? Usually, it's a way for males to display their strength and size. It's almost like saying, "Don't mess with me—I'm big and tough!"

Gorillas know how to get a point across! Thanks to their unique blend of sounds, gestures, and expressions, these apes are skilled communicators. From grunts to giggles, gorillas have several ways of expressing themselves. Learn a bit more about their lingo below.

PIG OR PRIMATE?

"Uh, uh, uh!" That's the piglike grunt a gorilla makes to demonstrate mild aggression. The pig grunt doesn't mean an ape is going straight into attack mode. It's a warning to other gorillas to watch out and, if necessary, step aside. It says, "Back off a bit. That's my food, and I don't want you to even look at it!"

WHAT'S SO FUNNY?

"Ha, hahaha, hahahaha, ha, ha." No, no one told a joke. All the same, it's not uncommon for gorillas to chuckle, especially if they're in a playful mood. Scientists say this type of laughing sound expresses joy, but it is also an invitation. A gorilla's giggle translates to, "Do you want to play with me?"

This baby gorilla was orphaned by poachers. After being rescued, authorities moved the gorilla to the Virunga National Park.

CHAPTER 3

Struggling to Survive

Fossils show that apes' early ancestors probably appeared about 20 million years ago. Despite having survived for this long, several species face a troubling future. Gorillas are often killed as a result of Africa's charcoal, lumber, or **bushmeat** trades. People also poach them to use their bones, organs, and hair in traditional medicines. Other illegal hunters slaughter gorillas for sport. They display the gorillas' bodies or body parts as trophies.

Infant gorillas may be sold illegally for up to $40,000.

No Place to Call Home

Loss of living space threatens gorillas, too. As land is developed for human use, these apes lose their habitat. People cut down trees for lumber and charcoal, as well as to set up farms and mines. This destroys the forests where gorillas live.

The construction of roads adds to the challenges gorillas face. Roads lead to a greater human presence within natural environments. They also make it easier for poachers to access the gorillas.

People often harvest bamboo, a common food for gorillas, from the forests.

Armed conflicts cause problems for gorillas and their habitats.

The Impact of Other Human Actions

Poaching and habitat loss aren't the only human activities that take a toll on gorilla populations. Some people kidnap baby gorillas to sell them as pets. These animals often suffer after being removed from the wild. They don't always receive the care they need to survive.

Political unrest throughout Africa creates further problems for gorillas. Buried explosives, called land mines, used in wars, injure and kill them. War also increases human traffic within gorilla habitats.

Ebola is not only dangerous for humans, but also gorillas.

Deadly Diseases

Disease has also devastated gorillas. Within the last few decades, a virus know as Ebola has probably killed 33 percent of the wild gorilla population. There are five types of Ebola. Four of those types make people sick, but all of them affect nonhuman primates such as gorillas. Ebola causes high fever and internal bleeding, which is bleeding that occurs inside the body. Gorillas also suffer from illnesses such as tuberculosis, a disease that affects the lungs.

Startling Statistics

At present, all gorilla subspecies are critically endangered. For some subspecies, there are fewer than 1,000 left in the wild. Even the most common one, the western lowland gorilla, has a population of about 100,000. Compare that to humans, who number 7.4 billion worldwide.

Gorilla Subspecies Populations

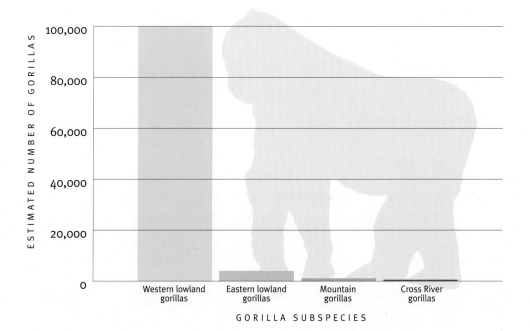

A caregiver holds
a four-month-old
gorilla as it drinks
from a bottle.

CHAPTER 4

A Chance to Change the Story

The future of gorillas is uncertain. Yet people have an opportunity to change that fact—and to make sure these majestic apes survive. Conservationists use many different approaches when it comes to protecting gorillas. At present, it is illegal to hunt gorillas in any countries where they are found. Though not everyone believes conservation laws are well-enforced.

Orphaned baby gorillas must be bottle-fed five times a day.

WWF workers patrol for poachers in Gabon.

Gorilla Guardians

Luckily, conservation groups such as the World Wildlife Fund (WWF) are doing their part to prevent poaching. They help local authorities monitor the health and safety of various gorilla populations. The WWF also assists rangers in organizing patrols to watch for poachers.

In addition, conservationists work with government officials in central and western Africa. They push for stricter enforcement of anti-poaching laws. This means fining or imprisoning any violators.

Safe Spaces

Protected areas such as national parks are also critical to gorilla conservation efforts. Government officials don't usually allow the natural habitats within these areas to be changed or destroyed. They limit the development of roads and buildings, as well as the clearing of trees and other plant life. As a result, gorillas don't have to compete with humans for space. Roughly 17 percent of wild gorillas live in protected areas.

Roughly 320 gorillas live in Bwindi Impenetrable National Park in Uganda.

Conservationists in protected areas often rescue and **rehabilitate** gorillas. They provide medical care to animals suffering from bullet wounds, breathing problems, and a wide variety of other issues. They also feed and nurture orphaned babies. In certain situations, rehabilitated gorillas are released back into the wild. Other apes require ongoing support. Such gorillas often spend the rest of their lives at sanctuaries.

Timeline of the Amazing Ape

ca. 20 million years ago
Apes' early ancestors first appear.

1847
Gorillas are recognized as a species.

1933
The movie *King Kong* comes out, inspiring a fear of gorillas; gorilla hunting increases.

Getting the Word Out

People don't always know about the threats gorillas face. So conservationists raise awareness through programs in zoos, nature centers, and schools.

Conservation efforts also address poverty in central and western Africa. Sometimes villagers turn to poaching out of desperation. Creating more job opportunities is therefore a positive step for both people and apes.

1994
During an armed conflict in Rwanda, 22 gorillas die.

2008
Researchers estimate the world's total wild gorilla population to be 100,000 to 200,000.

2005
Scientists observe for the first time wild gorillas using tools.

No Guarantees for Gorillas

It will take a lot of work to help gorillas escape extinction. Some conservationists predicted mountain gorillas would be wiped out by the end of the 20th century. Mountain gorillas didn't disappear, but how long will they—or the other three subspecies—last? Hopefully, with continued conservation efforts, these incredible apes will grace the African wilderness for centuries to come!

A troop of mountain gorillas spends time in a clearing in Volcanoes National Park in Rwanda.

Ape Advocate

Dian Fossey (1932–1985) was a conservationist originally from California who spent 18 years studying mountain gorillas in Rwanda. Fossey became famous for her interactions with these apes. This interaction allowed her to study up close their habits and how they communicated with one another. She also learned a lot about how the social structure worked within a troop. Fossey's work also raised awareness about how close mountain gorillas are to extinction. ★

CALLING ALL CONSERVATIONISTS!

Conservationists represent all walks of life. Some are scientists. Others are kids just like you! What can you do to help? Here are a few ideas to get you started:

"ADOPT" A GORILLA

Talk to your student council about hosting a bake sale or car wash. Donate the money you earn to the care of an orphaned ape. The operating costs of organizations such as Gorilla Doctors are expensive! In exchange, such organizations often allow people or groups to "adopt" a gorilla. (Don't worry—you won't be bringing a wild animal home. You'll probably just receive photos and updates on how your ape is doing.)

RAISE AWARENESS

Think about designing posters that feature pictures and fast facts related to the four gorilla subspecies. Ask to hang them at your school or community center.

PROTECT THE ENVIRONMENT

Write out a list of environmentally friendly decisions that protect gorillas' natural habitats. For example, be sure to recycle paper whenever possible. This helps save trees—and the forests where gorillas live!

INVITE AN EXPERT

Work with school officials to arrange for guest speakers who are experts on gorilla conservation. Contact your local zoo or nature center to see if they know anyone who's willing to visit.

Do Gorillas Belong in Zoos?

The debate about keeping gorillas in captivity is nothing new. Some people argue that these apes belong only in their natural habitats. Others point out that zoos protect gorillas and raise awareness about the challenges they face.

Which side do you agree with? Why?

Yes It's okay to keep gorillas in captivity!

Gorillas aren't safe in their natural habitats. They deal with several ongoing threats, including poaching, land development, and the dangers of living in war-torn areas. In zoos, they can socialize and reproduce in a more protected environment. When captive gorillas are ill, veterinarians are on hand to treat them. In fact, zoo gorillas have a life span of up to 50 years. (That's about 10 years longer than the life span of wild gorillas.)

Just as importantly, **zoos help educate the public**. Visitors have a chance to observe gorillas and learn more about why they're at risk of becoming extinct. Zoos, therefore, encourage conservation!

No Gorillas do not belong in captivity!

With so few gorillas in Africa's forests, it's not right to keep any in captivity. Plus, zoos don't always meet gorillas' social and space needs. In the wild, gorilla troops may have as many as 50 members. That is a lot of gorillas for a zoo to care for! In addition, a troop's dominant male often expects young males to eventually leave. In zoos, males must be moved to a new space or zoo when the time is right. A healthy environment also includes plenty of room to roam. Some wild troops have a home range as big as 16 square miles (40 square kilometers).

When zoos can't provide these features, **captive gorillas may become restless and aggressive**. Being surrounded by walls and unwanted attention from people can make this behavior worse. Gorillas should not be kept in cages!

True Statistics

Estimated number of gorillas (all subspecies) in the wild: Between 100,000 and 200,000

Estimated date when gorillas will possibly no longer exist within much of their current habitat: Mid-2020s

Total number of gorilla subspecies: Four

Number of unique sounds scientists believe gorillas make to communicate: At least 22

Typical life span of gorillas in the wild: Up to 40 years

Percent of gorillas' genetic code that is shared with humans: More than 98

Percent of the wild gorilla population that the Ebola virus has probably killed: 33

Percent of the wild gorilla population that lives in protected areas: Roughly 17

Did you find the truth?

F Not all types of gorillas are endangered.

T A dangerous virus is a major threat to gorillas.

Resources

Books

Dakers, Diane. *Dian Fossey: Animal Rights Activist and Protector of Mountain Gorillas*. New York: Crabtree Publishing, 2016.

Katirgis, Jane, and Carl R. Green. *Endangered Gorillas*. New York: Enslow Publishing, 2016.

Nippert-Eng, Christena. *Gorillas Up Close*. New York: Henry Holt and Company, 2016.

Visit this Scholastic Web site for more information about gorillas and to download the Teaching Guide for this series:

⭐ www.factsfornow.scholastic.com

Enter the keyword **Gorillas**

Important Words

bushmeat (BUSH-meet) meat that is obtained by hunting

conservation (kahn-sur-VAY-shuhn) the protection of valuable things, especially forests, wildlife, natural resources, or artistic or historic objects

deforestation (dee-for-is-TAY-shuhn) the removal or cutting down of forests

ecosystem (EE-koh-sis-tuhm) all the living things in a particular area

extinction (ik-STINGKT-shuhn) the permanent disappearance of a living thing

genetic code (juh-NET-ik KODE) the chemical basis of characteristics that are passed from parent to child and that determine how a living thing looks and grows

poachers (POH-churz) people who hunt or fish illegally

rehabilitate (ree-huh-BI-luh-tayt) to bring back to a normal, healthy condition after illness or injury

reproduce (ree-pruh-DOOS) to produce offspring

sanctuary (SANGK-choo-er-ee) a natural area where birds or animals are protected from hunters

subspecies (SUB-spee-sheez) a group within a species that contains related plants or animals

Index

Page numbers in **bold** indicate illustrations.

About the Author

Katie Marsico graduated from Northwestern University and worked as an editor in reference publishing before she began writing in 2006. Since that time, she has published more than 200 titles for children and young adults. One day, Ms. Marsico would love to go gorilla tracking in Rwanda.

PHOTOGRAPHS ©: cover: John Lund/Getty Images; back cover: Suzi Eszterhas/Minden Pictures; 3: Vlada Photo/Shutterstock, Inc.; 4: Steve Bloom Images/Alamy Images; 5 top: Raul Touzon/Getty Images; 5 bottom: Stan Osolinski/Getty Images; 6: Martin Harvey/Getty Images; 8: Gorilla Doctors; 9: Gorilla Doctors; 11: Cyril Ruoso/Minden Pictures/Getty Images; 12: Steve Bloom Images/Alamy Images; 14: Vlada Photo/Shutterstock, Inc.; 15: Danita Delimont/Getty Images; 16: Eric Isselee/Shutterstock, Inc.; 17: Terry Whittaker/Alamy Images; 18: Thomas Marent/Minden Pictures/Getty Images; 19: Arco Images GmbH/Alamy Images; 20: Mark Newman/Getty Images; 21: Bettmann/Getty Images; 22: Bildagentur Zoonar GmbH/Shutterstock, Inc.; 23: Arco Images GmbH/Alamy Images; 24-25 background: Jamie Farrant/Dreamstime; 24 left: Andrew Plumptre/Getty Images; 24 right: Stan Osolinski/Getty Images; 25 left: Konrad Wothe/Minden Pictures/Getty Images; 25 right: Andy Rouse/Getty Images; 26: Phil Moore/AFP/Getty Images; 28: Eco Images/Getty Images; 29: Stringer/AFP/Getty Images; 30: Dagnino Enrico/Getty Images; 32: John Moore/Getty Images; 34: Photoshot License Ltd/Alamy Images; 35: imageBROKER/Alamy Images; 36 left: Sabena Jane Blackbird/Alamy Images; 36 right: AF archive/Alamy Images; 37 left: ALEXANDER JOE/Getty Images; 37 right: Terry Whittaker/Alamy Images; 38: Nature Picture Library/Alamy Images; 39: Liam White/Alamy Images; 40 left: skynesher/iStockphoto; 40 right: Cathy Yeulet/iStockphoto; 41 bottom left: Image Source/Getty Images; 41 right: hillwoman2/iStockphoto; 41 top left: Roman Samokhin/Dreamstime; 42 inset: Cyril Ruoso/Minden Pictures; 42-43 background: Patrick Rolands/Dreamstime; 43 inset: Raul Touzon/Getty Images; 44: Eric Isselee/Shutterstock, Inc.

Maps by Bob Italiano.